NETWORKING FOR WRITERS

A FUN WAY TO SELL MORE BOOKS

LIZZIE CHANTREE

CONTENTS

NETWORKING FOR WRITERS

How to create your own bestseller support system.

Lizzie Chantree

❀ Created with Vellum

ABOUT THIS EDITION

Networking for writers is written and edited in British English rather than American English. This includes spelling, grammar and punctuation.

Image credits:
LemonTreeImages. Martin-dm.
Smrm1977. RawPixel Ltd. Diane Lomarde.
Pobytov. Jodie77. Bet_Noire.
Closeupimages. Doradobra.

ACKNOWLEDGMENTS

To my network of readers, writers and other creatives. Thank you for all your support, friendship and encouragement. It means the world to me!

BOOKS BY LIZZIE CHANTREE

Contemporary Women's Fiction

Babe Driven

Finding Gina

Love's Child

Ninja School Mum

If you love me, I'm yours

Launching in 2021: Shh… It's Our Secret

INTRODUCTION

I have always been fascinated by information and learning new things. Over the years, I've met lots of people who I now see as part of my 'network,' my group of interconnected friends and acquaintances. They have helped me to evolve into the bestselling author I am today.

I have had a very varied career path, and I believe that a lot of my success is due to the contacts I have made at every stage of my working life. These connections are fluid and change all the time. The links can reach across decades and the process ebbs and flows both ways. This book has been written in uncertain times, during the global pandemic, but even when people have been isolated and unsure, they have found new ways to connect, to reach out and communicate and to inspire each other with innovation and kindness.

I have written this book to help writers find their own network and learn how to communicate well with their readers and social media followers. I hope it will offer support to new writers, but also assist established creatives and writers, directing them towards new methods of establishing their writing brand and expanding their social media sites beyond recognition. The book is a way for them to explore and create their own ideas.

ABOUT THE AUTHOR

My name is Lizzie Chantree and I started writing novels seven years ago. I am now the author of five international bestselling contemporary romances. I hit both *Amazon*'s #1 Bestseller spot and #1 Hot New Release spot with my novel, *If You Love Me, I'm Yours*. I self-published my first three books, after turning down a traditional contract due to family circumstances (my daughter was unwell for many years but is fine now). My books regularly hit the bestsellers lists, even though I was completely unknown as a writer when I published my first book. I believe this is due to my network.

I started my own company at the age of nineteen, from a craft barrow in a shopping centre. This evolved until I was operating two retail shops and a wholesale business. I ran these for over fifteen years, which taught me how to interact with clients and customers. It also gave me an insight into business, which is why my fiction books are full of sassy entrepreneurs who get themselves into all sorts of mischief! Through these stories, I enjoy imagining what it would be like to run some pretty eclectic businesses.

I was voted one of the female inventors of the year by the Patent Office and Fair Play London, for my invention, Runaway Spray. It's a lipstick-size ladder or run-stop spray for hosiery. This led to me being invited onto TV and radio shows like This Morning, Open House with Gloria Hunniford, The Big Breakfast and the BBC World Service. I was interviewed by both the ITV lunchtime news and Sky News on the same day. This happened alongside being featured in many national newspapers and glossy magazines. It was all a bit surreal, to be honest. My first customers were the Arcadia Group and Superdrug.

Years later, I began writing as a way to reduce stress. I hid my first book in a cupboard for five years, until I found the courage to let it see daylight as my daughter's health improved. I was really nervous about publishing my first book, but I'm so glad I pushed myself out of my comfort zone. My books are full of friendship and laughter and are about women with unusual and adventurous businesses, who discover they are far stronger than they realise. I now work as a business/creative mentor in my spare time, I was a judge on the Shell Livewire Grand Ideas Award, and speak at seminars about networking and writing. I host multi-author book signings for other authors and speak at seminars about networking.

I also run a networking hour on *Twitter* each Monday evening, where creatives can chat about their businesses, writing and other endeavours. It's a wonderful place to interact and to begin to grow your own network. This networking hour, #CreativeBizHour, has been trending on and off for years. I get millions of timeline views during this one hour window each week.

Writing books is a lot of fun, but finding a readership can be exhausting and demoralising, even if you think you have a wonderful book that people will love. A network can help you to keep isolation at bay, give you support when needed and help you discover amazing contacts, some of whom might become friends for life.

In this book, I will talk to you about:

- How networking can help you as a writer
- Author branding
- *Facebook* groups
- Networking hours
- Hashtags for writers
- Your timelines

One important aspect of building a network is time management. I will give you tips on:

- How not to waste valuable writing time
- How to simplify your marketing plan
- How to make your marketing more effective
- Apps that might help save time
- Scheduling social media posts

Note: There are some links to apps in this book. They are ones I use personally, but I do not receive any money from mentioning these links. There are many more products and services out there, I just mention ones I have tried and that work for me.

. . .

Networking can be tricky, especially if you are shy, or lack confidence at times. When I wrote my first book, I was used to making retail and wholesale sales face to face, but selling a book you've written is different. It feels very personal and pushing it out into the world is scary. You may even suffer from imposter syndrome, and worry you don't deserve success or aren't as good at something as everyone else. Believe me, the majority of creative people I speak to feel that way. Being artistic can mean we are wonderfully sensitive to the world around us. This helps us in our art, but it can also make us doubt ourselves unnecessarily. At first, even the word 'marketing' scared me! Now I find it a challenge that I enjoy. What difference a year or two can make.

LET'S TALK ABOUT NETWORKING

I published my first book at the end of 2013, after reading an article on self-publishing. It was fairly new then and there was sometimes a stigma around it. These days, many successful authors publish their own books. Although lots of authors earn below the minimum wage, many thrive. There are growing numbers of authors who have some books that are self-published and some that are traditionally published. It's a big commitment for a publishing house to take on a book, and it involves a lot of work from both publisher and author to find success. There are a lucky few who might be able to sit back and just watch it happen, but most of the people you see in the bestseller lists have worked very hard to be there.

I had no social media following when I decided to publish my first novel, and nor did I know much about it. I had a *Twitter* account, but didn't use it actively until 2016 or 2017.

- I currently have 65.3k *Twitter* followers
- I average 1 million timeline views a month

- I have over 2.5k *Facebook* contacts on my author page
- I have over 130k unique monthly views on *Pinterest*. It's a completely different kind of interaction to *Twitter* or *LinkedIn* and has seen massive growth recently. My viewer figure was over 1 million, but you do have to create unique content and interact often or numbers will drop rapidly. This figure goes up and down regularly.
- I have just under 10k *Instagram* followers
- I have over 8k *LinkedIn* connections

I am not writing those numbers down for any other reason than to show how quickly you can grow your social media following and how those numbers can drop through inactivity. If I can grow my network in four years, so can you. I don't spend every hour of my day on social media. I manage to spend time with my family, meet friends for coffee and still write and sell books. Marketing your work can be time-consuming, but it doesn't have to control your life or leave you without enough hours in the day to write, or create content.

~

When I became an author, I attended free courses that were offered in my local community. A great place to find these is via local business networks, your council, or pages on places like *Facebook*. Most towns have community groups and they often mention seminars being held in the vicinity. Once I had found courses to join, I used the opportunity to ask the host or expert lots of questions. It's a good idea to have a few things you want to know scribbled down, so that you don't forget them. A way to start talking to other attendees that you don't know, is to ask them what they are hoping to get out of the meeting or seminar. You could also ask for a transcript of the seminar from the host, if there is one available. I took notes and listened to the advice. Not everything will suit you, but there might be a gem, or even gems, of information that are worth attending for. Networking is a way to increase your profitability, referrals, to grow your business or brand and to garner recommendations for your work.

Free courses to encourage people to network can range from tips on how to use social media, building business relationships, finding sponsorship or funding opportunities, for example. Check out your local business network, libraries and council sites, or ask your peers or a mentor.

Most of all, don't ignore a vital resource. You! The saying goes – *if you are looking for the person who can change your life, look in the mirror*. You are your own best advocate and you know your work inside and out. If anyone can let the world know about what you do, you are the best person to do it. You don't have to be an outgoing person or have a big social network to start building your own following for your work. You can begin by implementing a few simple steps and see what works for you. Unless you are very well known, your work probably won't sell itself, so expanding your network of contacts can help broaden your reach and bridge the gap between potential readers and your books, or your product and customers.

Networking is also about being brave, even when it makes your knees wobble with fear. A very high percentage of attendees at events want to meet new contacts but over fifty percent spend time with people they already know. Statistically, women tend to make fewer than half the contacts that men make, so let's reach out and build those connections. Lots of networking can be done online nowadays, which could be less daunting. Be strong and make the most of every opportunity, even if it makes you a little nervous. You never know who you might meet. I will talk a little later in this book about how chance encounters can open up opportunities.

HOW NETWORKING CAN HELP YOU AS A CREATIVE

Word of mouth is very powerful. Having a network of friends, family, colleagues, readers, business owners and contacts can give your work a head start and make it stand out from the crowd. Books, especially, can get lost in a sea of new releases. Thousands are published each day. What can you do to make your work fly off the shelves?

A good way to begin is to build a support network. This should be made up of people who would potentially enjoy your work and tell others about it. They might not directly buy your work themselves, but they could share it to their own networks, post it on their social media timelines or speak to people about what you do. This is still very valuable. Please do not ask your family members to be the first people to buy your books on *Amazon*, however tempting that is. *Amazon* will send alerts for your new books to the first people who bought your previous book and you want this to be avid readers, not your mum or your uncle Fred. You can tell your family about it yourself. Hold off, sit on your hands, eat the occasional cake, and distract yourself any way you can! It's difficult, as everyone wants to see sales straight away, but this will not benefit you in the long run. Amazon will look at these first customers and assume they are your target market, even if they really prefer a different genre generally, or are not avid readers and are just buying your book because they love you. This confuses algorithms right from the start.

Networks can be built through social media platforms, such as *Twitter, Facebook, Pinterest, LinkedIn, Instagram, Litsy* and more. But they can also be built via local or online groups, through friendships, people who work with you or anyone who has similar interests. Having a large group of people who do not appreciate what you do will not help you at all. Although I do have a fair-sized social media following, many of my connections are specifically interested in either books, writing, creativity, business or entrepreneurship. As this is what I do and write about, my network is valuable to me as a writer, and does not just represent customers, but mentors, friends, sounding boards and so on. If I had a following of people who didn't like my timelines (the places where I post content on social media seen by my account followers), it would be pointless to rack up follower numbers. It's better to have a smaller following that fits your brand or genre, than a big following who barely read your posts.

There are many ways to build a network on social media. A good way is to look at timelines similar to yours and follow a few people at a time. *Twitter* doesn't like people copying *Twitter* follower lists, so adding a few accounts you admire at a time is a good start.

Next is interaction. Jump into conversations, (remembering to be respectful) and let others know your account exists. You could look for people who are talking about a book you like, and join the conversation with your own recommendations, and comment on posts in your genre. This gets your brand and account known. If you want to, you can unfollow those who don't follow you back after a while, as they might not be interested in your content. People who don't follow you will not see your timeline unless you interact with them by joining in with conversations. But be careful, only join in when people are asking general questions. Don't leap into personal conversations. If you like people's content, even if they don't follow you back, then continue to follow them on social media. You never know when you might be able to become part of each other's network. Lots of high profile people never follow back, but they do still chat and network with their followers, which can be a lot of fun.

WHERE TO NETWORK

In this digital age, networking doesn't have to be done in person. The isolation that many of us have been living through during the pandemic has meant people have found new ways to communicate and work together. People have begun chatting in groups on apps like *Zoom* or *Skype,* and are being inventive about making new networks within their brand or business. People who were once in brick and mortar shops have moved their sales online, offering virtual tours of product shelves, and those who are not able to provide face-to-face services have made videos and podcasts.

Each day we are finding new ways to network, showing that you can market without huge costs and still generate a following and new customers for your brand.

Ask yourself why people should look at your work. How do they find out about you, and do you have something to offer them, other than buy-my-book posts? There are many ways to engage readers or customers in conversation, but the best way is to be genuine and not push them to buy. They know what they like, but are probably also often open to ideas that innovate or capture their interest in ways they aren't expecting.

Online and local groups are a wonderful way to interact with customers. I started my own group on *Facebook* as a way to connect with readers and other writers and the group has evolved into a place where we share reads and swap ideas. I ask readers to help authors with marketing and promotional advice, which gives avid readers an insight into the writing process. Everyone is supportive of each other and the members are all very important to me and are part of my growing network. We currently have around one thousand group members. If you'd like to join, Lizzie's Book Group, please do! There is a link to my group at the back of this book.

There are many great groups you can join on *Facebook*, but I'd advise against picking too many. The idea of a group is to interact. If you are a member of lots of groups, there is no way you will remember which ones you said what in, or which ones have promotional days. Be selective. Pick a handful of groups and really become part of the fabric of the group, as my members are. If anyone needs a shout-out or help with a particular issue, I put it to the group or help where I can. I also know that if I need something, they are there for me. It's a two way street. This was demonstrated recently when I created a post in my group, asking for bloggers to host a book launch. I soon had forty responses offering space. I put a lot of work into the group for others, but I feel that I can rely on many of them for help too. If you can't find the right group for you, then why not start your own? It doesn't have to have hundreds or thousands of members to be effective.

Local community groups are also wonderful places to connect. Councils often run free courses for locals to help their businesses grow – and writing is a business too. I have been on courses about *LinkedIn*, *Twitter*, branding and many other topics. Utilise the free facilities available to you. These are good places to meet up with like-minded people and to expand your network.

Libraries sometimes run groups. Book groups are obviously popular, but libraries are perfect spaces to meet up for networking or creating your own group environment, too. They hold creative days, seminars and book signings. Go to them and meet other book lovers and writers. Take part in library events, show you are willing to be part of the reading and writing community and introduce yourself to the staff. Enquire about holding book signings for your books, or about running seminars and ask if the library could invite their own book group members. Leave your branded bookmarks there for avid readers to use, if the library allows. They are a great advertisement for your books.

LinkedIn is known as a business network. I don't post there very often, but have built up over eight thousand connections. I don't accept every connection request, far from it, but I now have a *LinkedIn* network full of screenwriters, authors, readers, entrepreneurs, business people, innovators and people who post content that might be useful for my other social media pages, and vice versa. I don't have to search for material to use online, as I'm already linked up with lots of amazing people who are regularly posting content that interests me and will probably interest my network. Likewise, I post content from my other networks that might interest people on *LinkedIn* and be useful for their own connections. I often post my latest blogs and book news to *LinkedIn*. This is a professional space and some of the chat is about recruiting, but it's also a place to showcase your work history. You might find other creatives to work alongside here, as well as mentors who regularly post advice on different topics.

The same works for *Pinterest* and *Instagram*. I post content to make my readers smile. This is because my genre is romance. I like to think that my books make my readers happy and I try to do the same with my social media posts. Why else should they bother to share my content, or tell their friends? Their time is as precious as mine. You can easily make memes (images with text) for your pages, with free and paid programmes. *Canva* has templates for most of the social media sites and you can drop your text or book covers into ready-made designs. *BookBrush* is another great book design template company that is easy to use and has free and paid options.

TWITTER NETWORKING

Social media started out as a way for people to stay in contact with friends and family, but it has evolved into a means for us to share photos, videos and news, to engage with customers and build brands. I began using my *Twitter* account, @Lizzie_Chantree, a few years ago and it has grown steadily with genuine followers. I don't see the point of buying followers, as they would probably be robots. There are lots of ways to grow your customer base organically without having to spend money. It does take up a little time, but I feel the end result is worth it. Some people worry that social media platforms can be hostile places, but that really shows that generating your own follower base of like-minded people is worth the extra effort. Don't randomly follow anyone you can, just to get numbers up. Follow a selection of people who match your brand or customer base. Don't bulk follow, or *Twitter* will start limiting your account options.

A good way to network on *Twitter* is to join in with social media hours. These are often run by one or more people using unique hashtags. A hashtag is a live link or tag in a tweet, that makes it easy to search for a word or term. I started my own hashtag hour, #CreativeBizHour, because I wanted to engage with my followers and discover people with similar interests who might also enjoy my books. Remember, my stories are full of creative entrepreneurs who get into all sorts of scrapes, so there is a possibility that my networking hour guests might also enjoy my writing.

To start your own *Twitter* hour you must first find a unique hashtag that others aren't already using. Type in the word on *Twitter* with the # symbol before it and see if it is already in use. Running a hashtag hour takes a lot of dedication, as you need to create content for the people taking part and engage with guests using the hashtag in their tweets for the duration of the hour, replying to chat. I post questions every ten minutes to engage my audience, and use graphics like the one below, in different colours. I write a question for each tweet, add the hashtag and then the image. I schedule these questions using the scheduling application *Buffer,* and then I spend the hour talking to my network and engaging with their responses. It's great interaction. If you type the #CreativeBizHour hashtag into your *Twitter* search box, you will see all the latest or top tweets with the hashtag, plus find out who runs the hour. Me!

Without the hashtag in your tweets, there is no live link to the networking hour. The only people who will see your messages are your own followers. If you want to expand your reach, add the appropriate hashtag, i.e. #CreativeBiz-Hour, to each tweet and response to conversations, every single time you take part, but only during the time the networking hour is being run. Just add the hashtag to the search bar on *Twitter,* and it will take you to the top tweet using that hashtag. It will also show you photos people are posting, and any videos that may have been uploaded. If you use the hashtag, your tweet will be seen by anyone else searching for the same hashtag too, and you might gain new *Twitter* followers, or get retweets for your post. Retweets enable your post to be seen by the retweeter's followers, who might also like your books or content and click your links. You are likely to have similar interests to those in the networking hour you choose, so you could follow some other participants too.

It's not professional to start a networking hour and then not show up to run it every single week. This would not look good for your brand and would possibly upset the people taking part, causing people to drop out or unfollow your social media page. Some *Twitter* hours have multiple hosts. This means a few people take it in turn to run their hour and have set dates to organise the hashtag hour timeline. This can be very helpful, but also has its own problems if the hour gets very popular and one host has different ideas from another, or if one person is shouldering the majority of the responsibility. Choose your co-hosts wisely.

Some new networking hosts will retweet every post which includes their hashtag, to help it move up the trending charts. This might work for a while, but they are likely to get banned by *Twitter* for over-posting. This could upset followers who are then not able to join the hour, or other followers who don't want to see so much content. If a person has a few hundred followers, they will see most of the posts from the people they follow and repetitive retweeting could flood their timeline. Instead of seeing a handful of genuine, interesting tweets about the topic, they would see a barrage of posts being retweeted. This might make them hit the unfollow button in droves. Be mindful of your current followers when setting up a networking hour.

If you'd like to join in with anyone else's hashtag hours, including mine, add the hashtag to your tweets during the set hour. Tweets with quality photos in them get far more traffic and retweets. Don't forget to add your book or work links.

An example of a #CreativeBizHour tweet:

Hi #CreativeBizHour How are you tonight? If you are looking for a new book to stay up late with, check out my latest novel, *If You Love Me, I'm Yours.*

This tweet would accompany a *Twitter* graphic for my book and a universal link to help people find it on *Amazon.* A universal link is specially designed to take a person from the UK to the UK *Amazon* book page, but will direct someone from France to the French book page on the *Amazon* site, and someone from the USA to their own *Amazon* site.

The secret to *Twitter* is collaboration. If you are active there and join in with the community, customers and business connections are more likely take an interest in you and your work. If you just drop a tweet and run, and this does happen a lot, then why should anyone bother taking notice of you or your work? It might even make people feel indifferent to your writing or creativity. This isn't to say that you have to spend your day in front of your computer or phone, it just means it's a good idea to chat now and then, and respond to messages.

People sometimes ask me why someone else's tweets achieve more traction, but if they looked back at their own timelines, they would probably find that it's all information about themselves and no one else. If they clicked on someone with an active timeline, however, they would probably discover that they chat to their followers, interact, retweet others and offer support. This doesn't mean you should retweet all the content you can find. That might annoy your followers, especially if they don't follow many people, as your posts would appear regularly. If someone has a lot of followers, it's harder to keep track of every tweet and the account holder will only see timeline posts when they are looking on the application and that have been posted recently. This is why some people post the same tweet time and time again, hoping to catch a customer's eye at some point. Once again, this might bore users with smaller follower counts, as they could see every tweet you send out. Keep your posts on topic, and don't over-post.

Do not ignore your customers. Readers love chatting to authors, and many authors love getting feedback from readers, too. If someone on *Twitter,* or any other social media timeline, mentions that they love your work or have told someone about it, do respond. Ask for feedback and say thank you for their time. Query what they liked about your writing. Make the most of this opportunity to build your readership. Word of mouth is extremely valuable and it costs nothing, other than your time and theirs. I have met so many wonderful people online who are active readers. They are a big part of my network and shout about my books from the rooftops, when I have a new novel to launch. For this I am very thankful. They are absolute stars.

Join in and be sociable. I meet a lot of people on my networking hour who are reticent and don't like to jump into conversations. This is ok too, but people won't know about your work, unless you tell them. Social media isn't about tearing people down. Lift others up. What can you say about someone else's work that will make their day? They could remember your words and might then share your work when they see it. You get out what you put in. You can't expect your work to walk out of shops on its own, so having a backup network is a good way to help your self-confidence sprout wings.

Look for topical hashtags that relate to your business and add these to your tweets to widen the audience that sees your posts. This type of topical hashtag is searched for regularly. Here are some examples of a few that are good for writers:

#WritingCommunity #Amwriting #Writers #WritingTips #WritersCommunity

Also check out daily trends and add some to your book tweets:

#MondayMotivation #TuesdayMotivation #WednesdayWisdom #ThursdayThoughts #FridayFeeling

Share your fears and successes too. Most people have down days and it can be intimidating if you are always posting about successes. Be realistic on your timeline and share failures as well as triumphs. This helps followers see that you are human. Then they will engage with your timeline and know you are still learning too. People might be interested in what you had for breakfast, lunch or dinner, but they are more likely to want to know about your writing or creativity. Make your posts relatable to your audience.

~

Twitter list building is a good way to create or find content for your own timelines at a glance. *Twitter* gives you the option to build lists. Click on your profile on *Twitter*. You will see the word 'lists'. You will see a small blue list icon with a + sign, towards the bottom right-hand corner of your phone, or the top right-hand corner of your computer screen. Click this. You will be asked to create a new list. Give your list a title and a description. You have the option to keep the list private so, if you don't want others to see your curated lists or the content of your lists, tick the private box. I keep most of my lists private. I do have some that I've let others see and copy, to help them start curating their own content.

Make lists of *Twitter* pages that show regular content on the theme of your list. For me, it might be, for instance, publishers, authors, creatives, entrepreneurs, family life, current affairs, or anything that fits my brand as an author and creative mentor. When I am looking for new ideas to post and have a lull in my own content, I can easily click on one of my lists and find lots of tweets on each topic, with very little effort on my part. Other people have added my *Twitter* feed to their own lists to utilise the content the same way. This, in turn, can help you find new followers – and you are supporting others by sharing their content too.

On *Twitter*, you have the option to pin a tweet to the top of your timeline, by clicking the little grey downward facing arrow in the top right hand corner of the tweet. It says 'pin to your profile' if you click it. Some creatives like to keep the same tweet pinned for a long time, so that the retweet numbers get higher. I prefer to have a fresh tweet pinned every few days. This means that anyone visiting my page can see a tweet to retweet at the top of my page. If they visit often, which many of my followers do, they can find fresh content to share. I'd rather have varied tweets that people can easily share, than one tweet with a high retweet count that people can't share again. This is just my personal preference.

When I visit pages I like to stop by regularly, it can be time consuming to have to scroll through their *Twitter* timeline to find content to share. Sometimes I move on without finding anything if I am in a hurry. I am far more likely to share content to my own social media followers, if the tweet is fresh and pinned to the top of a page. If I have shared it before, I can't share it again, although I can retweet my own tweets once more after I have posted them. I often do this to refresh my post to a new audience at a different time of day.

FACEBOOK NETWORKING

Facebook is a wonderful place to link up with like-minded people. There are many groups where you can chat to other creatives and writers. You just have to find the right one for you. When I first became a writer, I joined so many *Facebook* groups that I took half an hour to just scroll through the names. This is counter-productive. It's better to be a member of a smaller number of groups and to interact and actually make use of your contacts there. If you spread yourself too thinly, you'll end up exhausted and wonder why no one knows you or your work. Marketing can feel like walking up an endless hill and can also be very isolating. It doesn't have to be, and you don't have to be uber-confident to join groups. You do need to pop by and engage with other members from time to time.

Marketing shouldn't mean you have no time for writing or socialising. Both are a creative lifeline. If you schedule and plan your time effectively, then the networking you are doing could be enough.

Many authors have their own *Facebook* street team groups

for their books. To start a street team, you create a new group on *Facebook* and invite your team members in. These are people who you feel will support your work and help spread the word about it. Make it feel like an exclusive group. These teams are built up with readers who are happy to push out news to their own networks, when you have a product or book to launch. These groups are often small, but can grow in size too.

You will need to supply content that is interesting to your members, like updated book graphics for them to use and share on their own social media pages and blogs, promotional images and written information. Make them as excited as you are about your upcoming book release. Show them what is wonderful about you and your work. Focus the group on the genre you write in and update it regularly with posts that are on brand and relevant to your work. Keep it entertaining. By this I don't mean you have to make them laugh, but post fresh and interesting content about your work that leaves them hungry for more news. You could offer your street team early copies of your books, bookmarks, book vouchers, free short stories or sneak peeks of your novel before anyone else, to make them feel special.

This might sound exhausting, but small groups can be very effective and don't require as much work as larger ones. You could choose to post once a day or even once a week. I post a few times a day to my *Facebook* book group, because I interact a lot with my members. This works for me. It helps my brand and network grow, plus it's a lot of fun, but it isn't necessary when you're just starting a group. I offer my group content to assist with marketing for writers and I also encourage reader and author interaction, which builds connections.

With a *Facebook* timeline (the part of your profile page

that updates with your information), you can only have one profile page that can send out, or accept, friend requests. If you are an author, you can't have a personal profile page that can accept friend requests, and one in your author name that does the same for readers. If *Facebook* discovers that the same person has two personal profile pages, they can shut either or both pages down without notice, and you might lose your content forever. Because of this, I chose not to have a personal *Facebook* profile, so that I could accept friend requests from readers and other creatives I have not always met personally, but who enjoy my work or the posts on my author business page. You can, however, have multiple business pages from one personal profile. The business page does not have friends, but people can 'like' the page and follow it. If your personal page is set to public, people can also follow you there without you having accepted a friend request, so check your settings and make sure you are happy with them. Do your best to keep your network full of like-minded people, the same way you would with any other social media pages. You don't have to accept every friend request.

With your business profile, although it's great to get 'likes' and 'follows', the best way to widen your audience is via comments. *Facebook* likes interaction and focuses on meaningful posts. This means that adverts or links are not as highly valued as comments, and will not reach as many people's *Facebook* pages. Responding to a comment on one of your *Facebook* posts within an hour can boost that post's visibility. The conversation – the visitor's comment and your reply – means the content has interaction, which makes it more valuable. It is then boosted to the timelines of more of your friends or social media followers. So please remember to check back and respond to comments on posts you have made.

As with all social media pages, don't spend hours watching dancing dog videos, however cute they may be. Set times for writing and times for marketing and social interaction, and stick to them as best you can.

OTHER SOCIAL MEDIA – INSTAGRAM AND PINTEREST

I am beginning to use *Instagram* and *Pinterest* more regularly, as they are a wonderful place to network, but my writing time has to be a priority. Lately, I have been running writing buddy sprints in my book group at set times, and this does make me write more words down, faster, which in turn frees up more time to post news about my writing and books to my other networking channels. Writing buddies are people you don't work with directly. They are other writers that you arrange to work alongside, either online, or in a café, library, or another agreed work-space. You have set times to meet and work, and then you stop work at another set time, to see what you have achieved. This can be done with two people, or in a larger group. Sprints tend to be for a shorter period of time, hence the name. They are a great way to help you focus on writing and that in turn frees up time for marketing.

The same rules apply here about keeping your *Instagram* and *Pinterest* pages on brand and appropriate to your genre. If someone stopped by your page, would they know you are a romance author, a mystery writer, or that you have a theme for your books? This could be trickier to manage if you write in more than one genre. You might want to think about setting up different accounts for each. The problem is that this adds to your workload. If you are constantly posting jokes, but you write about deep issues with sombre themes, this could confuse a potential customer who is following your account for a daily dose of funny memes. I'm careful to stay true to my writing style. My pages are full of fun about being a writer, the stories I write, the places I write, and how my customers might relate to my books.

My *Instagram* followers have come to expect my genre from my timelines. If I post about my books, they know what they will be about. I have built a network of book-loving and writerly followers, and I enjoy seeing their posts too. I take time to comment and interact with my followers' posts. I also follow people who post about books, writing and entrepreneurship, as that is what interests me and I can easily jump into any conversation. Making comments on *Instagram* is very important, as this often results in someone else looking your page up and becoming part of your network too. They then might like the look of your work, and buy it or tell their friends.

~

Pinterest is a very different type of social media channel. It's about aesthetics. You are showing people your taste and engaging in visual communication. I share things I enjoy on my boards. My network can see at a glance that I love books and they can also check out my *Pinterest* boards about my own novels. I show my book covers, what my characters look like, and also reveal the theme of my books in case they'd like to know more about them. Each pin I make myself has a link embedded. If people like the image and click to find out more, it will take them to my book page for that novel or to my *Amazon* author page. My *Pinterest* page has grown rapidly, after using some tips I have learned. Within the first day of implementing them, my website views rose by one hundred and fifty percent and one of my books was pushed back onto the bestseller lists.

Making pins is very easy. Follow the instruction on your *Pinterest* page. Add an image, then a description, and make both very clear. You will be asked for a destination link at the bottom of the pin. This is where the customer will be sent to if they click your pin/image. This could be your *Amazon* book page, your website or blog address. Make the image relevant to the post that you are sending the customer to. It's not a good idea to have a photo of a beach party and then send the customer to your website that has crime novels, or a photo of a beautiful dress, that ends up linking to a blog about writing. *Pinterest* check that photos match the destination link and that customers are not being mis-lead, so be clear with your photo and link target destination.

My *Pinterest* page can be found at: Lizzie's Pinterest page if you'd like to pop by and see how I run it. I also design my own memes and add them. I stay on brand and they are about writing or are designed to make my readership smile. These pins all link to my *Amazon* author page or my website. This means people who click the links can then follow my author pages or blog posts and they also join my network of readers and writers.

The book pin I made below has my website links embedded into it. I did this by simply adding my website URL (www.lizziechantree.com) to the pin description, when I set the pin up on *Pinterest* and added the image. People who like book memes are likely to be book lovers and might also enjoy romance reads from my own book list.

My tips for a great Pinterest page:

- Keep the page on brand.
- Add boards and pins to your page that relate to your writing. I have varied boards on my page, but the main ones are about romance, top reads, networking, writing tips, author branding, writing memes, things to make you smile and so on. Add new boards regularly, but do not spam, which means don't post too many at once. Think about how much time you can commit to *Pinterest* and be consistent. With your *Pinterest* pins, it's better to

post one pin a day, than twenty in one day and then none for a month. Some people post between ten and a hundred pins, spaced out regularly during a day, but there is no point doing this if you can't maintain this flow, or if you are not posting original content. The key is not to overwhelm your audience and grow your page organically over time.

- I now post four pins evenly spaced out in a week with my website link in them. They have fresh images with new titles that are different from the week before. I mix these with up to ten pins a day from other pages that I like on *Pinterest* and re-pin those with *Tailwind,* which is a social media application. Once you have an active page, *Tailwind* will start suggesting pins for you which relate to your content, so you don't have to spend time searching for it. I also make up to four book related pins to send readers to my *Amazon* page with my book covers on them. I post these to different boards throughout the week. When I stopped doing this, my *Pinterest* views fell from over 1 million to just under 100,000 and my website statistics dropped too. I'm currently building it back again.
- Make a selection of your own pins for your books. *Pinterest* makes this very easy. You can drop a photo in and they will ask you for destination links and a description. Then you can publish your pin straight away or schedule it via *Pinterest.* An alternative is to design your own pins using templates on sites like *Canva.* You then drop the design into the photo space and add links the same way.

- Title each of your pins individually with relevant descriptions and make all of the names different. Computers will read the pin titles and 'image100002345' will get lost as there are probably millions of those out there. 'Thrilling Crime Reads Pin' by (your author name) will be seen, read and thought of as original content. This boosts the pin and might generate a new customer base, as more people will see your pin, or be encouraged to follow you as a new content creator.
- When creating your own pins for *Pinterest*, **Write Your Pin Titles Like This.** Add capital letters for the start of each word. Do this for titles only. For example, **5 Bestselling Romance Reads**.
- Think of keywords. When you use the search bar in *Pinterest* for words relating to your books, what shows up in the drop down menu? These are the most searched-for terms relating to your search. Use these keywords in your own pin descriptions. This will make them rank higher as they match the most popular search terms. If you search 'crime reads', for instance, you might find the most searched terms to be 'crime reading list', or 'must-read crime books'. In your own crime read pin, you could add your book cover or a picture of someone reading with your own headline, and write a description like this:

Discover some amazing new crime reads to add to your must-read crime list! Reads by (author name). Ultimate thrilling reads.

- When you click the crime novels reading list, for example, you might see hundreds of pins. Look at the most popular ones. These are the pins on the top few rows. What are the pins called? What are their titles? Can you make a pin with your own heading that uses some of those keywords?

- Once you have clicked the heading you want from the search bar in *Pinterest,* it will also give a list of keywords along the top of the page in coloured blocks. These are words that people have searched for, associated with the heading. Add the relevant ones to your pin description. Don't just list them. Make a proper description for your new pins with the terms relevant to your work or the page you are directing them to. Some people use hashtags in their pin descriptions, but I like to write relevant descriptions of my pin image and destination site and the words themselves form keywords.
- Add your blog or website book page to the links, if you want more page views from crime read lovers who click the link, or add a universal book link to your buying pages. You can create universal links at sites like *Booklinker* or *GeniusLink.*
- I have made pins that link to my blog page so readers can see all my current books, but I have also tailored them to the topic of my current blog post. If I write a post about how to start a book for new writers, I might make a pin with the title, Tips for Writers, with a subheading, from a bestselling author. I would then add a link to the related blog post and a description with keywords I have found in a search for something similar to the title of my pin. This then sends budding writers to my blog, which is full of content to help writers and is also a meeting place for readers.
- Mix it up with pins from other sites. I do this

because it creates other interest for my readers and *Pinterest* followers. I'm not a builder or an architect, but I have my dream writing barn and love to post photos about that. My viewers might also be interested in looking at ideal writing spaces. Finding new ways to engage your readers is paramount. I could write some blog posts about dream writing barns, then add a pin linking to my blog to the board. People who like looking at writing barns could then easily stumble across my own content and enjoy my books, blog or website. It's about creating a tight link between all of your social media followers and your brand.

- *Pinterest* is a very visual site, as I've mentioned, so make your pins interesting and people might pin them to their own curated boards, which in turn widens your audience and places your work in front of new potential customers.

YOUR TIMELINES

How do you communicate your writing ethos to your network, without hard sell or over-posting on social media? A good way is to make sure your book pages and websites are updated regularly. Do your timelines represent your most current work, or are they outdated? Do they show readers at a glance what they would be getting, if they clicked your book links, without you directly asking them to buy your book? If not, what can you do to make this happen?

Networking is not one-sided. It's about helping each other. Don't drop in to your timelines once, and expect everyone else to do the work and share your book news. Why should they do that, if they don't feel they know you very well? A good network is one that interacts regularly and offers mutual support. I often share news, reviews, business updates and ideas from the people who show me support with my writing. Why wouldn't I? They tell their networks about my writing and mentoring, so I return the favour as much as I can. People will not know you have shared their work directly from another website or *Amazon* page, unless you tag them into your tweet or post by adding their @name. Don't do this excessively, as it might seem that you are shouting for attention, but most accounts, however big, will enjoy word of mouth and notice your posts, if you are friendly and positive.

Someone who writes romance and romantic comedies, as I do, would confuse customers if they posted photos of anything scary or overtly political. My books are not part of that world. They are written to help people have fun, smile and enjoy some relaxation with my feisty entrepreneur heroines and their families. If I wanted to post anything controversial, I could easily keep it to my own personal timelines and away from work platforms (not that I post content like that anyway). Obviously, if you write political thrillers, satire about the world around us, or any content related to current affairs, then that is different and some opinions might fit your brand.

Posts on timelines are called stories for a reason. Are you telling the story of who you are and what you write? It's always worth considering how much of your personal life you want to share on your timelines. Some people will want to share all of their news and some will curate it, sticking with writing and books, and moving away from personal details. You have to do what is right for you.

Interaction is key with timelines. With *Facebook* or *Instagram,* as I've said a post is boosted if you respond to any interaction on your post within one hour, so it's well worth watching for interaction after you have posted, but timing isn't as critical on other social pages. Sites like *Buffer* can post for you, or *Facebook* itself now has a scheduling feature. *Buffer* posts out the content you have provided, on your behalf, at set times. You must create or search out content for your timelines that fits your writing brand. You don't need to post every hour, a bit of interaction throughout the day should be sufficient. Four to six posts a day should be plenty on *Twitter.* One post a day for *Facebook* and *Instagram* could be enough, but people do post more regularly. For *Pinterest,* you can post several pins in one day.

Space tweets evenly throughout the day. *Buffer* will offer you fixed times to tweet, at the optimum time for your timeline. These are the times that the application has deemed to be the most popular times of day to post, due to views and page visit data. This is only available on the paid version of the application, though. The free version of *Buffer* offers you the chance to set up to ten scheduled posts a month, which is great for new users. The pro version offers space for up to one hundred scheduled tweets a month. Over-pinning on *Pinterest* can be interpreted as spam, so pin effectively and at different times of day. Followers there will see your posts, either if they happen to check in at the time of posting, find your pins in search results, or look at your page directly.

You can repeat content on your *Twitter* timeline, but if you are using scheduling applications, they won't let you add exactly the same content more than once. Make sure you change at least one word in the repeated content, or alter a hashtag in the text of the tweet. Most social media sites don't like repetition. They sometimes look for posts that promote mental health and wellbeing and you might see these posts naturally boosted. You could talk about how writing has helped you make friends or colleagues, how it's motivated you to stay positive, or even the downside of working in the public arena.

Time management

. . .

Time management is important to ensure you make time for both writing and marketing. Establish a schedule and eliminate distractions where you can. A good place to start is to make a list of goals you want to achieve each day. Reward yourself for completing your list, or move tasks to the top of the next day's list. Use your networks to work towards your goals. If you have a problem with *Twitter*, for example, is there someone in your network who is proficient on social media who wouldn't mind answering a quick message, telephone call or email from you with some advice? The bigger your network, the more people you will have to draw on. Mentors are a big part of the writing and creative community, so finding yours, or becoming one yourself, can be a real boost. It might also be worth considering if you are spending time on tasks that you actually need to do. Are you wasting precious writing or creative time on projects that are not important in the bigger scheme of things? What can you do right now to set that balance straight? Put aside tasks that make you procrastinate, or draw your attention away from your writing goals.

AUTHOR BRANDING

What is an author brand? An author brand is the image you present to your customers across all your platforms, both personally and via logos, photos, book covers or creative graphics. You might want to create the graphics yourself, or hire a designer who has been recommended by others. Ensure you have a written or printed pricing quote, for the work that has been agreed on. You will need an author profile image, or a company logo, and a short description of your work that you can use across your whole network, including your website, blog and social media pages.

The first thing to think about is the genre you write in, or the message you want to convey for your business. For me, the key words are romance, comedy and entrepreneurship.

Do you have an author brand? If not, think about creating one. It's worth giving a lot of thought to it, because this is often the first impression customers have of you and your work. Pulling together an author brand might feel scary if you are not a graphic designer, but with technology today, it can actually be done for free, or on a small budget. If you want to pay a professional designer to do this for you, check their references first. The best place to find a good designer is to ask other authors whose branding you admire. Recommendations are a great way to find people to work with.

Why is branding important to networking?

When a reader first hears about your work, they might search for you on *Google,* or try *Amazon* or other bookstores online. People can have a very short attention span and you need to grab them quickly. How will they recognise your pages, genre and writing style, within the first few seconds of visiting?

You can easily take a good quality author photo on your phone these days. Ask a friend or family member to take one for you. Let it show your personality, but keep it simple with no distracting backgrounds, if possible. This will make it easier to recognise you on blogs and websites. Most blog hosts and people making enquiries about your books with regard to promoting them, will ask for an author photo to be sent across.

Things to think about:

- What genre do you write in?
- Is this easily recognisable from your social media pages?
- Does your branding stay the same across all of your social media sites?
- Who are your ideal clients and how can you attract them to your pages?

- Do you have a good quality author photo?
- Help customers recognise who you are and what you write.
- Do you have a media kit on your website? Media kits are explained further in this chapter.
- What can you post to your timelines, to show people what they would be getting if they picked up one of your books?
- Make sure your *Amazon Author Central* page and any other book site author pages are up to date.

The *Author Central* page is the page that customers click onto on *Amazon* to find out more about an author and their writing. Add your author biography and author photo, and links to your website if you have one. Your book covers will also be shown here with links to buy them. I often go to an author page on *Amazon* or another book site to find out more about an author I like and it's frustrating when this is left blank. It's also a wasted opportunity to connect with a potential customer.

Customers might also want to check out your personal timelines on *Facebook*, by searching for your name. If your page settings are set to public so that anyone can see your content, be sure to think about what you post there too. The main header photo on my social media is a simple deep blue background, featuring all my book covers. This identifies my writing genre as romance reads, using imagery that people can recognise straight away. It's simple and effective. You will see this same header on my website, *Twitter* page, *Facebook* pages, *Instagram, Pinterest, LinkedIn* and anywhere else I can post. If there is no space for a header on the social media platform, then I publicise the books in posts. Because of this consistency, a customer looking for my work can recognise my page, anywhere, in seconds. Once again, you can set up your own images in applications like *Canva*, where there are pre-set sizes for headers and posts. You can also try *diybook-covers.com*. If you click on *3D Mockups* on the drop-down menu on the right-hand side of the main page, you'll find steps to turn your book cover into a beautiful three dimensional image. Copy this into your design template on another graphic programme site or use it for *Twitter* and *Facebook* posts. *AllAuthor* is another site which sets up free and paid banner images that you can drop your book covers into.

The main thing is to keep your branding simple and to apply it across your pages. Use a template if you find design a bit daunting. If and when you update the design, do it for every page you run.

Here are some examples of my branding and book covers.

These are examples of 3D mockups and my header

banner. I also use my tagline (*Bring that holiday feeling home*) and I add my website address and *Twitter* name if it will fit into space and it isn't already in the bio or page description.

Media kits

Media kits are useful tools for authors and creatives. They are a great way to simplify information and make searches for your work easier. A media kit helps newspapers, magazines and blog hosts to access your data in one easy place, without having to scour the internet for your book, author, or product information. I have my media kit on a page of my website: LizzieChantree.com

A media kit can help you to reach new audiences and expand your network. It makes it very easy for others to add your details to their own articles and websites, and assists readers in discovering the links to buy your books and find out more about your work. It helps your author or creative brand to look professional.

In my own media kit, I have added all my social media links and some fun facts about me as an author. That way, journalists or tour hosts can grab content easily without having to contact me multiple times, adding to their busy workloads.

A media kit should include:

- Your author photo. Make this an easily downloadable size. I have a few different-sized author photos on my computer, so I can send the right size when requested. Label your photos for ease of use. For example: **Lizzie Chantree Author Photo**. This makes it simple for media contacts or blog hosts to find your work, amongst thousands of author photos they might have stored. Do this with your book cover photos – and, in fact, all your photos! Searching through pages of photos to find the right one can be very frustrating for a tour host or journalist. This also helps with *Google* rankings. If a photo is labeled, for example, img100012, it will be seen as anonymous duplicate content, and the article it is included in will drop down the rankings. Label photos correctly and simply.

- List one book at a time.

Underneath each book, add:

- Book photos. Separate photos of eBook and paperback.
- Book title.
- Genre.
- Publication date.
- Pages.
- Book buy link.
- Price for both eBook and paperback or hardback.
- Book blurb.
- Social media links.
- A short Q&A about yourself.

GET WRITING

One of the things many writers forget when trying to build their network is to **prioritise** writing time. Marketing can seem so overwhelming that it might feel like a heavy burden that has to take precedence over everything. This quote always makes me remember what has to come first:

And also,

Work out set times for marketing, and stick to them as best you can. This helps prevent marketing and networking from becoming too much of a pull on your time. We do need to network and create a readership, but without finished work to promote, we've got nothing to talk about anyway. A really great way to sell books is to write more books! People love a series, and will often purchase the next in the series if they have just read a book and enjoyed it. Make sure you have links in the back of the first book, to take readers directly to the buy link or pre-order page for your next book. Also add the blurb, to let them know what they will be buying.

I procrastinate, but I'm also very efficient. This sounds like a complete contradiction, but I allow myself time away from work to daydream, meet friends and chat with family or colleagues. I even squeeze in watching a few of those funny dog videos! But I also schedule my marketing and writing time so that these two elements are prioritised. It's amazing how much you can do in one full hour. Many people organise all their marketing in one hour a week. I set one hour or more aside every weekday, and have a checklist. My working day might look like this:

- 8.30am. I take ten minutes to check social media feeds and make notes, or say good morning to followers.
- 9am-10am. One hour of writing. Target 500-1,500 words.
- 10am-11am. Design a handful of new *Twitter* ads/*Instagram* photos/*Facebook* graphics, or schedule a selection of tweets/posts. Resize the designs to fit each specific social media page, or use *Canva* design pro to resize. You still have to move the text, but *Canva* automatically changes the graphic size. Put these images or photos in files that are easy to find on your computer and are clearly labelled, as this will save a lot of time later.
- 11am-12.30am. Post to *Twitter, Facebook, Pinterest, Instagram, Litsy* or any other social media site. Check responses and chat. Use the same post for all social media to save time if you want to. If social media channels seem time-consuming, pick one or two. As I've said before, it's better to interact properly on one than to spread yourself too thinly.
- 12.30am. Lunch break. Quick check and respond to comments on social media feeds. Maybe do a few star jumps, sing out loud to annoy the family and scare the dog, or go and meet friends.
- 1.30pm. One hour of writing time, if you still have writing targets for the day.

- 2.30pm-4pm. For me, this is school run time. During lockdown I have also spent a lot of time baking and learning new skills with my family during this period.
- 4-5pm. One hour of writing time, marketing or updating blogs.
- Evening. Family time, watch television, run my networking hour, write – or rest!
- Rest is very important to creativity. This doesn't mean spending half of your life dozing on the couch, unless that makes you incredibly creative the rest of the time (and it does work for some creatives). It means that writing, creating and marketing all take their toll on our mental health, though they might boost it at other times. Build relaxation into your day and reward yourself for your achievements with treats where possible. This might be a walk with the dog, a chat with friends or a huge slice of chocolate cake in front of your favourite television programme! A huge slice of cake every single day might not end up being ideal, but time to yourself is. Give yourself credit for all you have achieved each day. Any words on paper for your latest writing project are a great achievement.

This schedule is a rough guide and can be juggled around to suit my day. It needs to be fluid to fit round family life. Every one of us is different, so make a schedule of your own, if it helps you concentrate on your writing or creative time. Some writers hate working to a schedule, so it's up to the individual to decide if they are getting enough words written each day. Some authors would be happy producing a hundred words a day, but others can manage thousands, so work at your own pace. Don't panic if you don't reach your targets, just move things around the following day and start afresh. Each day is a new writing challenge!

During the pandemic lockdown, I began a writing buddy/sprint system to encourage other authors to keep writing and to stave off isolation. We started and finished working at the same time, then checked back in to see what we had achieved in a short space of time. It worked wonderfully, not just for the people who joined the buddy/sprint sessions, but for me too. We all began at 10.30am, and then reported back on my *Facebook* book group on at 11.30am, to state our achievements. It wasn't about competing over our word counts, but about our own personal goals. It was a way to encourage each other. Some people used the time to write blog posts, edit manuscripts, proofread, or schedule social media. It helped us motivate each other to get words or ideas written down. The writers didn't have to share word counts at the end of the sessions unless they wanted to, so hopefully they didn't feel any pressure. It was about teamwork and using our support network of other writers to keep us focused and make us concentrate for one hour. It was amazing to see what everyone achieved. I wrote this book! You can't edit a blank page, so any words written, or ideas noted, were an achievement and I had happy writers who didn't feel so isolated. It was also a lot of fun.

Is there anyone you can start writing alongside? It could either be someone you sit with in a coffee shop or library, or perhaps an online friend who would like support or a challenge. Then you can work together for a set time. This is a wonderful way to make yourself write regularly and builds trust and communication with your network of authors. Who knows what you might go on to collaborate on in the future? Build those connections, and get writing! If you don't like to write in a set timeframe, you could arrange to connect with writer friends at the end of the day, or week, and share achievements the same way.

MARKETING PLANS FOR WRITERS AND OTHER CREATIVES

Having a marketing plan can make it easier to check at a glance what you have organised for the coming weeks or months. There are books you can buy or downloadable sheets available online that can help you plan your days. It's a good idea to have a 'month in review' list, where you can check back to see what has worked, or not worked, with advertising or events. You can list which strategies succeeded, or failed, and work on how to improve them. You can also list advertising campaigns booked, note the dates they ran and the number of responses, or downloads and sales, and therefore be able to tell if they are worth doing again.

Check your visibility. Most social media applications will have an analytics tabs. Look at them regularly. They will tell you what is working, or not working, on each social media page. *Twitter* has categories like top mention, top media tweet, most retweets, number of impressions and top follower each month. It also shows how many new follows, profile visits and tweets you are receiving. Most other social media pages offer the same insights. Use this data to understand which posts work best, which are engaging with your audience and who your top influencers are. How can you engage with those influencers?

Compare month to month, measuring against how much you engage with your social media followers. If your numbers drop rapidly, it might mean you are not posting enough of the right content at the right time. Publish consistently and keep thinking of ways to network quickly and effectively. Can you write four blog posts, and schedule them every week for a month? Then you can forget about them for a while. Don't ignore any engagement on these posts though, as these interactions are often from your fans or core readership. The same applies if you are being featured on someone else's blog. It can be frustrating for a blog host when they take the trouble to set up a post and the author does not come back on the day it goes live and engage with the audience or share the post. It's a wasted opportunity for the author, as they could meet new readers and contacts via the comments on the blog post. The blog host might not invite the author to be featured or interviewed again, due to their lack of engagement.

For your own pages, think about whether you should post the same content across all your networks, or change it up. I'd advise changing some of the content, as it's likely that fans of your work will follow all your social media channels and they won't want to be bombarded with the same information. Consider how long post content needs to be. Long and detailed posts might bore your readership, but could help with search engine optimization, so find a middle ground. I tend to use a minimum of 300 words. Bullet points and easily scannable headlines can help break up a lengthy post.

Use popular keywords and search terms in your blog text to help boost rankings, especially in subheadings, but make sure they are relevant to your post content. If you have outside domains (web addresses) linking to your website, this can also help your SEO rankings. Internal links are ones linking back to your own articles. External links describe an instance where you post a link that is outside of your own web domain, or takes a reader to another site. Adding high quality and well trusted external links can increase your digital footprint. Your willingness to add valuable links and resources can demonstrate that you want your readership to fully explore a topic further, rather than holding them on your own site. This is a way of showing you care about your readers.

Most website visitors stay for mere seconds, to decide if the content is for them. Make sure you interest them with an image and attention-grabbing headline, first, and then offer useful, simple content. Add book links unobtrusively to every post. Easy post ideas could be top tips, things your readers don't know about you, how you write, when you write, your favourite reads, and your pets as writing buddies or inspiration. Remember to keep all posts on brand.

Things to think about in blog posts:

- Interesting and useful content. No waffling.
- Photos at the head of the article, even if you also have them further down the page. This translates well when people repost, repin or share your article.
- Make blog posts fun and interesting, or useful. Don't post sales posts about your book all the time, but do this occasionally.
- Backlinks. Can you add a backlink to another of

your previous blog links in the text? Don't add more than one per post as this can be confusing. Backlinks are a great way to show readers of one post more of your content, and raise page views. A backlink is simply a link to a previous post. You highlight a word in the current post, and add a live hyperlink which leads to an older blog post. This will offer the reader another article they might enjoy on the same blog in one click. This in turn improves your site visibility on *Google* and moves you up the page rankings.

- I would advise keeping any affiliate links to the end of your blog posts. They should also be on brand or be linked with your genre. I post links from high street bookstores, fashion brands, romantic holiday breaks, and content that relates to my books. If I started advertising fishing equipment, tents or DIY, it might make my readers wonder what was going on. You can join up to sites like *Awin* which will allow you to post affiliate links to monetise your blog. You have to apply to advertisers and become accepted, but advertisers can contact you too, which is a great compliment. The advertisers supply the images, links and the html code if you need it. To use the code with *WordPress* sites, you simply add it to your blog post, by clicking the html tab in your post and copying and pasting the code they give you to the end of your article. The image will magically appear when you turn it back to the text-ready view. This may be different with other platforms.
- Have content ready for other bloggers to share your work too. That way, if you get a request from

someone in your network, you don't have to panic and you can choose from a body of work.

Ideas for content:

- Character interviews. Posts where you interview your own characters or another author's characters, to give readers a different perspective on a book.
- Travel guides using the setting of your book.
- Host a giveaway of your books.
- Explain why you write in your particular genre.
- Show your own writing space. Readers love to see where writers write!
- Share inspiring quotes.
- Post news about something exciting that is coming soon, like a cover reveal.
- Q&As.
- Host an interview with a creative guest.
- Post tips.
- Ask questions.
- Tell your readers how you got started in writing or your creative field.
- Share three things they might not know about you.
- Post photos that inspire your stories.
- Post content that relates to *Twitter* hashtags. #MondayMotivation
- Share losses or failures to show you are human.
- Share successes.
- Share books you love to read.
- Show your creative inspirations.
- Share book groups you love.
- Thank your followers.
- Ask: *would you rather?*

- Show how you unwind after writing or creating.
- Share inspiring news.
- Post something educational.
- Promote your work.
- Share how you came up with your character ideas.
- Share a customer story or book review.
- Post photos with readers.

MARKETING MADE SIMPLE

Marketing doesn't have to be difficult. Believe me, I have tried many methods, and sometimes failed miserably. I have learnt from this and gone on to try other ideas – with great success. I am also a firm believer that you are your own best asset. You don't have to spend a lot of money on marketing. It can be done cheaply and effectively. It does help a great deal if you have design skills, though. But if you don't, don't worry. There are many programmes and applications out there which can help you. Many of them have free options which will enable you to make basic book or writing graphics very simply.

Spending more time on marketing than writing is counter-productive. Make your book as good as it can possibly be, as you can't expect good sales from a book that people don't want to read. Simplify your marketing plan to make time for writing and creative inspiration.

Have you thought about:

- Setting goals. What are your weekly writing and design goals?
- Checklists. These are simple visuals of what you have achieved, or want to do.
- Social media updates. Rather than panic over the amount of work to do, decide on how often you want to post to each account and schedule some of it. But be aware that too much scheduling can make timelines impersonal and turn readers off.
- Have you designed a selection of book graphics that you can use to promote your work on social media? Most authors have these. Spend time making book memes or graphics that you can reuse time and again. Seasonal graphics are useful too, depending on your genre. Halloween, Valentine's day, Christmas, Easter.

- Do you pop onto your social media pages throughout the day, to chat to readers? Try to do this regularly. Keep it to a few minutes per slot so that it doesn't eat into writing time.
- Keep your timelines updated regularly. Schedule time for this. Do not try to fit it in at any old time of day or it will take over.
- Keep up to date on current trends and hashtags, and find out ways to include these in your marketing.
- Content is key for making your timelines interesting. Make sure they hold value for your followers and encourage them to like, comment and most importantly share your posts to friends on their own network. This will boost your *Facebook* ranking.
- A good way to engage followers is to ask questions. Posting a photo with the question often generates more interaction with your network. Questions also help build new relationships within your follower base. You can find out more about each

other, and your likes and dislikes. Questions and answers are a way to fast-forward relationship-building with your network. Add questions to pictures to make your images stand out. Respond to questions on your timeline as this will also boost your rankings.

- If you are planning to pay for marketing, ask around and see what is working for other authors. There are lots of different networking groups for author marketing on *Facebook,* but remember only to join one or two, not hundreds.
- Keep a detailed plan of what you have paid, when you have paid it and what the results are. This is key to understanding what had been successful and what hasn't. Ask your network of writers for ideas and plan marketing together as a group offer or exclusive.

After you have simplified your marketing plan, there are ways of making it even more effective. You can make an Excel spreadsheet of social media performance, noting dates scheduled, post details, links, shares, follows, comments and your answers. You can also list your adverts and promotions and state the results clearly in columns. This makes an easy reference for further promotions. At a glance, you can see what has worked and what hasn't.

You could also have a dedicated social media planner, where you mark down each day which posts you have scheduled or made, and which have received the most comments or link clicks. This tells you what you audience are looking for. Make use of the *Twitter* analytics page I've mentioned before, where you can see how effective your tweets are, which follower has their own biggest following, how many clicks were made and so on. This will help you reach out and grow your network. It shows what your followers are looking for and what new followers might enjoy. Most social media pages have an analytics tab. Click this and it will show you a wealth of data about how your posts are performing and how your network is engaging. Use this to find out which types of posts are worth repeating and which ones to drop.

PROMOTIONS

There are many ways to utilise your network to help promote your book or brand. A strong network will lift you up and spread the word about your work. But don't forget, a network is a two-way street and it is also about what you can do for them. If you think people will do your work for you for free, think again. You need to offer them something in exchange for their engagement. Your content must make them want to share your promotions or book releases. If you have a travel book, for example, you could offer advice in your posts about different parts of the world, or show exciting and exotic photos for readers to enjoy. If you write in the thriller genre, you could tell gripping short stories or post podcasts with book readings.

Keep reading other people's blogs, and offer to contribute. Blogging is hard and hosts are often looking for fresh ideas and content. Ensure that the content you send them is professionally presented so that they can copy and paste it straight onto their blog, and don't forget to include great visuals. I know not everyone is a graphic designer, but most of us can present professional looking images, without huge costs, using the sites I've already discussed like *Canva*. You can also take photos of your own books on your phone, if it has a camera, or ask a friend to take a photo of you holding your books. Send your marketing posts to blog hosts in plenty of time, so they are not having to rush to fill the space with someone else's book if you are late. Their time is as valuable as yours.

No one is saying marketing is easy. But sometimes it's the people who don't put in the work to promote their writing, who wonder why their books don't sell. Marketing doesn't have to take over your life. Build a network of book lovers, authors and creatives around you, and then support them. Many of those people might, in turn, support you. If you expect it, they could become annoyed, but if you are gracious, encouraging, and open with useful advice and tips, so they get to know you, then why wouldn't they want to find out what you are doing next, and tell their friends? They'll do this in the same way that you'd be interested in what they are working on, and offer to share that too. Networking is about finding your group of likeminded people. Once you've done this, you have a great foundation relying on word of mouth – an amazing way to have your work communicated.

With paid advertising, I would advise you not to pay for visibility alone, as it is so short lived. It might make your book jump up the rankings initially, but the majority of the time it will end up straight back where it started a week later. Work out exactly what your aim is. Do you want to be high in the rankings, are you looking for profit, for newsletter sign-ups, reviews, or launch visibility? *Amazon* algorithms don't favour sharp sales spikes. Organic sales over a period of time maximise your visibility on *Amazon* after your promotion, so a 'little and often' strategy might be a good idea, to keep your book in front of customers in the long term. This means your book has a good chance of staying on a high rank, and will then continue to sell without marketing. This happens with series, or if you've written a few standalone books. A customer who has downloaded your first book and loves it, often wants to read more from the same author and buys another.

~

Giveaways are an exciting opportunity to expand your readership, for limited output. They can be organised in many ways, but something that works for me is posting a photo of one or more of my books, then adding text to a tweet to explain the giveaway. The tweet from me might look like this:

- Asking readers to tag friends means your books will be introduced to more potentially interested readers. For giveaways, you must have a link to a landing page on your website with full terms and conditions for the competition. This includes start and end dates and times, which countries the competition is open to, plus how many prizes there are, including the information that there will be no monetary alternative to the books or prize. You may not want to post books all the way to the other side of the world. For a *Facebook* giveaway, you must also state that the giveaway is not endorsed by *Facebook* and you are not allowed to ask people to 'like' the post. You can ask for a comment, social media follows if you have included links, or for readers to share the post on their own timelines. This kind of post can garner hundreds or thousands of responses, and helps boost your rankings and widens your network. You must announce the winner on your website or blog competition page, and inform the winner themselves at the close of the competition. Post about the winner on your website and social media pages and make them feel special. In turn, they might tell their wider circle of friends and family about their prize and the author.

- To make things easier, you could set up a spreadsheet and allocate entrants' details a number each. This data must be kept safe following data protection laws. Make the drawing of the prize a lot of fun and build expectation with a random number generator, which can be found on *Google*. This draw of the winning number can be made live on *Facebook,* or you can make a mini video and post it across social media.

Other promotions

Free short stories are a way to generate interest from your website subscribers and reward their loyalty. Stories can also be offered as a way to encourage newsletter sign-ups. They give readers a taste of your writing. Hopefully, they will then look up your published books and go on to enjoy the content on your blog, in your newsletters and on your website, and tell their peers and family. Newsletter swaps with other authors are also a way to share audiences and find new readers. Places like *BookSweeps* are often used by authors to grow email lists and social media following, and encourage new newsletter sign-ups. They work by running multi-author book giveaways, where readers join your newsletter in order to enter the competition. Authors pay a fee to take part, and offer two free books to the winner of the competition, to say thank you for entering. This can add hundreds or thousands of new readers to your email list and helps to find responsive readers in your genre, who may be on the lookout to buy new books. This promotion is very easy to participate in, as *BookSweeps* guides you through the whole process and even offers ready-made graphics to use. You can share these with your network as soon as the promotion goes live, while *BookSweeps* share it to their own subscriber list full of book lovers. *BookSweeps* also offer a variety of other sign-up promotions.

Facebook book hops

Facebook hops are a way to broaden your reader, or customer base and add to your network. A hop is when a group of people agree to post on a set day, or days, of the week. They then invite their combined readership, or follower base, to 'hop' between the pages. Customers are encouraged to leave comments, share posts and click links, for the possibility of exciting prizes. I have had almost a thousand comments from a *Facebook* book hop, and it is once again all about interaction. If you post and run, people won't come back to your page. There is no motivation when they don't know you or your work.

Usually one or more authors a day will be posting, and you all support each other's work by sharing on social media. You each post about your own book, but the hop often has a theme, for example, holidays or thrillers. You keep the post very short, ask a question which readers can answer, give a review or a quick character profile, and offer a prize that can be won at the end of the hop, in exchange for comments or GIFs to be posted below the original post. Always add a photo of the hop graphic, if you have one, so that readers know they are on the right page. You should also include a photo of your book cover and the prize you are offering. Blog hops often have a main prize that the group has contributed to, and individual prizes for each author post. You must include the competition's terms and conditions and state that the hop is not endorsed by *Facebook*. You can add links to your blog page or website leading to the terms and conditions, if that is easier.

As with giveaways, You **can't** ask for *Facebook* 'likes', but can add four or five links, which people can click on. Each entrant can be encouraged to click more links, to gain more entries into your competition. You might ask them to follow your *BookBub* page, or help with blog post shares, *Amazon* author page follows, sign up to your newsletter or anything else which will help you.

BookBub is a huge promotional site which sends out newsletters to its customer base of avid readers, when you have a free or discounted book to offer. You have to apply and pay for a promotion with *BookBub,* and it is very selective. Having followers on your author profile on *BookBub* might or might not increase your chances of being selected, but it does mean that your followers are notified of any updates on your account and of new books when you release them. Asking for *BookBub* follows during a *Facebook* hop is a great way to gain wonderful readers as followers.

I have found that the majority of blog hop followers are amazing and love interaction. They want to find out more about you and they will click most, if not all, of your links and follow you across all platforms. These are avid readers who love chatting to authors. You can find organised blog hops by joining *Facebook* groups that run them, or start your own with other authors. Once again, ask your writing network for recommendations for groups who host blog hops, or start your own.

Build a close relationship with your readers or fans. Share insights into your writing life, and treat them like they are part of an exclusive group.

Newsletters and blog shares are good ways to keep up interaction with your network. You can offer incentives at this point, too, which helps boost other bloggers' pages and builds your readership from their blog followers, who are already book fans following book-related blogs. It's great for the host to be able to offer a free signed book, a free short story, or even a branded mug or bookmark. It doesn't have to be a huge free gift, but might help build your readership if the winner loves your work and buys more, or tells their friends.

Discover what works for you. Build relationships. Turn readers into super fans, and show them why your network is a great place to be. It's about teamwork and mutual support at all stages, even when you are working alone.

Other promotional ideas:

- Share your story.
- Invite other authors onto your blog.

- Run promotions with other authors.
- Reviews. Use them! Add reviews to your marketing material, to show readers why others liked your books.
- Always make it easy for readers to leave reviews, by posting links on your networks.

Try new ways of marketing:

- Add calls to action.
- Add links and ask people to use them. I favour the words 'learn more,' or 'shop now,' as a call to action. Test some out to see what works for you.
- Newsletter sign-up links can be added to posts, promo links and review links. *BookSweeps* can help you build up your newsletter sign-ups.
- Create a tight circuit between your book and website. Have links to your website on your *Amazon* author page and links to your books on your website.
- There are many free website sites where you can create beautiful author sites for free. Places like *Wordpress* (www.wordpress.com) have basic templates that are simple to add books and text to. There are many other sites, but this is the one I use.
- PR. Use your network to send out press releases. Cross-promote with other authors and bloggers via each other's newsletters. Send your press release out to magazines, radio stations and newspapers, especially local ones. You never know who might be looking for content.

THE FRIENDSHIP NETWORK

Networking can be as simple as having a coffee with one individual. It is all about person to person, not business to person. We don't want our network to stay on one type of social media, we want them to visit our author pages, book sites, blogs – and buy our books. The purpose of a good networking post is not just to chat about yourself, but to engage your readership and add value to their day. Talk to your network about what inspires your work, share articles that might interest them, make them laugh, ask for their input and offer advice. Listen to what they are saying. Add a hook to grab their interest, be it an interesting headline or something that builds their expectation that something really exciting is about to take place, like a book giveaway.

Missed opportunities

. . .

Networking isn't just about sitting in a room with a huge group of people and wondering how many of them you might actually manage to speak to. It can arrive in many forms. One good contact can be worth twenty tenuous ones.

On one occasion, I went to an awards ceremony and was too nervous to speak to anyone other than the people I knew. Afterwards, writers I admired asked where I'd been, as they would have liked to meet up. My own lack of confidence had held me back and I could have kicked myself for wasting an opportunity to talk to people I look up to.

The next time I was attending a big awards ceremony in London, I was determined to push nerves away and to talk to people. I met a really lovely lady waiting outside the cloakroom. We chatted about our families for a mere five minutes, as it was Christmas time and school Nativity plays were being rehearsed all over the country. Later that evening, the lady I spoke to won the main award. I was thrilled for her and dropped her a brief message on *Twitter* to congratulate her. From this one small meeting grew a wonderful connection which has helped both our businesses, and widened our network in ways we didn't expect at all from that first chat. She is such an inspiring woman and shares many of her ideas and inspirations with her network. I feel very lucky to have met someone who is creative and so supportive of other woman. It also led to me being involved in the launch of her next business event. I received an exciting order for signed books, which were given as a welcome gift to every single one of the event guests, which in turn meant many new readers seeing my work. I was also invited to do a promotional video about my author journey to be played during the evening. Push yourself out of your comfort zone and say hello to others. You'll probably find they are as nervous as you are.

On another occasion, I was setting up for a big book

event I was hosting. I was outside the hotel where the event was taking place when a man came and said hello. He was painting the exterior of the hotel and owned a scaffolding business. He gave me his business card and we began chatting about the fact we both always have business cards with us. He told me that he'd met the hotel owner whilst working on another job and he'd given her his card. She'd remembered him and booked him to revamp the whole hotel. We then talked about my book event and he said his daughter loved to read novels, so I, in turn, gave him my own card, with my book covers on the front with my buy links, to pass to his daughter. You never know where you might meet a great contact. Always, always have some business cards in your bag or pocket. They are an essential networking tool and can be made simply via *Vistaprint* or other sites for a minimal fee.

If you are really nervous about networking, then take friends or family to events. That way you don't have to go alone and they might also enjoy the day out and meet new people too.

GENERATE YOUR OWN CREATIVE EVENTS

If you can't find a network that's right for you, you could think about creating your own. I decided to start running my own multi-author book signings called *AuthorsAt...* after helping another author I admire to create an amazing event, as we had been discussing book signings in my book group. I really enjoyed it but it was a long journey to get there, so I decided to begin my own book-themed day, nearer to home. My event was a lot of work, but the effort was worth it. I now have contacts in my network with local councils, hotels, musicians, artists, other creatives and more. It also led to me meeting the people running the Essex Book Festival. They then booked me to speak at the Festival about networking for writers. I was also asked to run seminars and workshops on starting and running book events, by other groups. This has led to me being contacted to run *Zoom* seminars, creative mentorship groups by the council and to write articles for magazines.

There is such a wealth of creativity locally to me, that with my multi-author book signing, I really wanted to shout out about writers and artists in Essex and share a bookish evening with the community, in a free event. At this point I was often asked, *why work for free?* I don't usually, but on occasion, it proves worthwhile. My *AuthorsAt...* event was free to authors taking a stand, and free for guests to attend as well. Many thought this was a bit strange, as I didn't make money from the event, even though it took a lot of time and effort on my part – but it was my way of saying thank you to my local community for supporting my writing career. A lovely bonus was that it gave me the opportunity to meet lots of new people in my industry, many of whom are now friends and part of my network. Those contacts have opened up many new work opportunities for me.

- If you don't want to run an event on your own, team up with others, but make sure job roles are clear, to avoid confusion.
- Cultivate relationships with venue staff, the media, local businesses, local creatives, book groups, libraries, catering firms, writing groups and councils.
- Go to open mic nights, poetry readings and literary gatherings, where you step up to the microphone and speak in front of a group, or watch others share their work. These are likely to be full of likeminded people and some might make good contacts for you in the future. I wouldn't advise going somewhere you aren't sure about on your own, though. Take a friend!
- Make use of the time before and after events. This is a great opportunity for informal chats. Many people rush away, but others linger to make the most of every connection.

Events are a really good place to network. With my *AuthorsAt...* event, I invited twenty-six authors to attend. I didn't advertise at all. My network spread the word. I was fully booked with amazing authors within forty-eight hours, including USA Today bestsellers, award winners and independently published writers. I made sure there were different genres involved, to attract a variety of guests. I was really lucky that I found support from local community. People were happy to publicise the event, as it was a fun way to meet writers in the area. This in turn helped local writers to build their readerships. Writing events can really create new opportunities if you take the time to mingle and make contacts.

After this one event, I was invited to participate in radio interviews for the BBC, I was offered the chance to work alongside the local council, and met councillors who attended the event. I was also invited onto blogs and booked for future speaking gigs after I did a short talk at a council-run seminar during the day. I also searched the internet for local events happening at the same time, and linked up with Essex2020, who were organising lots of events to celebrate the local scientific and creative community. This in turn helped me get invited to a networking evening, where I met representatives from *Google,* Newsquest, The Essex Book Festival, Local Council, Southend Libraries and Essex University, as well as local art groups and creative networks.

I had no idea all of this would happen. I had only planned a small community event, but it grew beyond anything I'd dreamed of. We had hundreds and hundreds of visitors on the day, stretching into the evening. We ran free workshops throughout, with the council and other authors. Small ideas can grow wings!

This promotion worked through word of mouth, because people helped each other. It was teamwork. Each author participant shared news of it through their own social media channels, which helped it grow. That was one of the conditions of the free stand and the authors were all keen to make the event a success too, as they also wanted to support the local community. During the event we had blackout poetry for people to try, funny book memes dotted around to amuse our guests, a flash choir, a local magician presenting book-themed tricks, and local artists who worked in the movie industry showcasing their work. This was obviously a huge event, but you could start small and build up over time. Two or three creatives working together can produce amazing results. I gave a lot of time and effort to my event for free, but it also helped people to hear about my work and gave me a chance to chat to local readers face to face. It didn't cost me anything to run the event, as the hotel donated event space and the entertainment joined us as a way of making new contacts for their own businesses. The hotel was fully booked for the evening, due to our event, and we all had an amazing time, with sales, enquiries and new additions to our networks.

~

During an event, give people a chance to tell their story and open up to you about their own writing or creativity. A shy person might be your next amazing business contact. Be patient, as everyone is busy with their own lives and you might have to book an appointment to talk to them at another time. Be inventive about events you might want to run and think of ideas why people might want to be part of it. Don't invest funds you don't have. Bartering is still a good way to find opportunities. Can you offer the hotel, venue or catering, something in return for their participation, like social media marketing for a short while, or a post about them on your website or blog? If you are nice and engaging and not pushy they will remember that. Ask for referral letters if you did a good job at an event, as these can pave your way to even bigger things.

When you attend events, have pre-planned answers to obvious questions like, *what do you do?* and *how experienced are you in your field?* as this can help to keep nerves about talking to new people at bay. If you are a new business or author, tell them why you set up or started writing, and the experience you might have that contributes to your field of expertise. Be a good listener and ask questions. The conversation might flow more easily than you think.

Networking is a good way to stave off isolation, especially in creative jobs where many work from home. Plan to run or attend online events if you are unable to travel. Play to your strengths. Consider doing speeches on your specialist subject – even if it's scary!

Another way to network is to hold workshops, or question and answer sessions. You can do this to small or large groups. I began with giving talks about my writing to local women's groups, and have been lucky enough to be invited back. Other invites to new events have come through word of mouth. Schools run many events and are often looking for specialists in a subject to come in and talk to students to assist their learning on a subject. Having a contact in a school office or on the parents' association is a good way to find out what they are looking for in terms of writing or creative talks. Some clubs and events have funds to pay authors, some do not. This is something to be negotiated before you agree to attend.

Make sure you get there with enough time to set up and practise your speech, knowing what your topic for the day is.

Visual prompts are often a good idea during talks, to help engage your audience. You could use a *PowerPoint* presentation, distribute hand-outs or have piles of books ready for people to look through – and hopefully buy at the end of the session.

Don't forget to look after yourself. Plan rest periods and ways to revitalise your creativity. I once went to a seminar where the host said he and his wife planned their business on a model of four full working days, with Friday off each week for a rest and family time! They have managed it well and now have a very successful brand. We are not all the same, we work at different rates, so don't push yourself beyond your limits and stress yourself out. Take networking at your own pace, and to suit your lifestyle. There are a lot of tips in this book, but if you start with one or two and dip in and out, using it for reference, then you won't feel overwhelmed. Creativity also needs play to grow. The key is to be kind to yourself to let creativity flourish, but also to try new outlets for meeting connections to market your work.

If you can't get out and about, there are many online networking communities. Check out recommendations from other creatives first and don't spend money on services until you know them well. Most services for book marketing design or scheduling offer free samples, allowing you to try the services out for a limited time. Add notes to your calendar to cancel them if they are not suitable – especially if you have to sign up with a credit card and start paying after the free trial month.

Keep in touch with your network. Nurture it. Volunteer in groups, be helpful, but also know when to say no. I use a trick where I say that I will have to check my diary before committing to anything. It gives me time to walk away and consider if I have the time and energy to attend or participate in an event. My writing time will always come first.

Be kind to yourself. Knowing you are all at events for the same reason can often help you replace anxiety with a feeling of satisfaction. Pat yourself on the back for your courage in attending. One of my author friends loves speaking and is brilliant at running seminars with huge audiences, due to his popularity. I'm sometimes really nervous about things, but I gently encourage myself to embrace my fears so I can expand my network and meet new people.

TO SELL OR NOT TO SELL?

Book marketing and signings or other events are not always about how many books you sell on the day, however strange this might sound. They are a golden opportunity to meet readers and other authors and to make connections with event organisers, venues, councils, and other contacts which will be useful in future.

Some readers don't want to buy paperbacks at events, but might go home and download your eBook instead, which could push you up the *Amazon* rankings. This has happened to me multiple times and causes a sales spike after an event. I once had a stand at a book event and sold one copy, which made me feel really sad and knocked my confidence. But at the end of the event, the venue manager told me he was starting a book group and was looking for a first read. He also needed authors to come in and speak to the book group. At another event I had one customer, but he bought one of each of my books for his wife, as she collected signed books. She became a loyal reader of my work. I also met a receptionist at a very quiet event who was starting a book group.

She loved my books and said she would recommend my stories for her group's first read.

Don't always view times when you don't manage to sell as wasted opportunities. Look around instead. Who can you network with?

- Use all events as networking opportunities.
- Make use of every minute.
- Chat to the hosts.
- Make connections with other stand holders and businesses.
- Talk to local book bloggers at book signings and ask if you can appear on their blogs.

Hard sell isn't always the way forward. I had a tweet picked up by *Microsoft* because I mentioned that a member of my family did a *PowerPoint* presentation to try and persuade me to buy her a hamster, including how pocket money could be used for bedding! There were no hashtags in the tweet at all, as it was just a fun post to my followers to make them smile. *Microsoft* sent me a picture of a hamster made out of icons, saying she deserved that hamster! We then ended up tweeting back and forth until **two** hamsters were bought, with a palatial cage. One of our miniature hamsters is called Micro. I have never been sent so many cute pet photos by my *Twitter* followers in my life! That one small post created a wealth of content, engaged my followers and expanded my network with hundreds of retweets and thousands of timeline views.

Widening your audience doesn't always happen immediately. It can take years to build up a loyal following and fan base, or it might expand in ways you never expected. It can really enrich your life and fill it with fun and excitement – if you are willing to put the effort in. Don't forget to make the most of opportunities presented to you, or to create your own. Book sales won't be handed to you. Find your readership and engage, engage, engage!

Some ideas for new content without shouting about sales could be, quick tutorials, asking questions about your followers' reading habits, short videos or book readings, sharing fun facts about your characters, creating a 'how to' video, posting reader photos with your books – and anything that brings your readers into your writing journey and makes them feel part of your team.

Social media can swallow you whole

Social networking can be exhausting. Take care and stay mindful that your writing is the priority. Always be aware of setting time aside for your writing and fit marketing around that. Social media is a big part of a marketing plan, but it is about being social, and not burning yourself out so that you have nothing left.

Social media is also supposed to benefit our mental health and help us create a community of friends and associates. If you find a post offensive or not to your taste, don't retaliate, just block the account or mute the timeline. This can easily be done in your social media settings. That way, you are building a community which is good fun and lifts your mood, without adding stress. You don't need to set an account to private to do this, just use the filters available. I tend not to follow back private accounts, because I assume they want their content to be private, but still want to interact with mine. That's fine too. It's personal choice. Many private accounts are full of friends and family and posts about them. It's unusual to find a business account that is private, as this defeats the purpose, but again, it's personal preference.

For social media:

- Add calls to action.
- Prioritise.
- Use set times and stick to them.
- Schedule, sparingly and effectively.
- Keep posts on brand.
- Enjoy yourself.

SHOW THE WORLD WHO YOU ARE

Why should someone buy your books over someone else's work? Try and think about what your USP (unique selling proposition) is? What makes your writing stand out? It could it be your genre, style of character, time zone, or maybe the fact it's on trend with current news. My own books are all about strong female entrepreneurs. The covers all work together and are easy to spot. Ask yourself how a customer would know your work from another writer's? How can you convey this simply and effectively? Stick to strong themes, or see what is selling and simplify your marketing.

What are you good at? Think about your customer base and work out ways you can use your own skill set to offer content they might enjoy. Who are your customers, or ideal customers? What is their gender and age range? These are important questions to answer before making sure your marketing is going in the right direction.

What can you do for others to make them understand your work better? Be generous and share knowledge. Don't be a wallflower, however appealing it might be. Find your network. If you don't know something, join an online or local course or teach yourself from the variety of free or paid facilities online. You might be surprised how many topics are available. I was watching a *YouTube* video a contact told me about, on lighting for people who offer online seminars. I was astounded at how much difference the right lighting can make to the quality of a live book chat and this raised a discussion in my book group. Open up new avenues for your business. Set up podcasts, *YouTube* videos, speeches, or find other ways to reach new audiences and present them as professionally as possible. Try things out at home first to see if they work before posting them online. You could use editors like *iMovie* to edit your videos and book trailers. There are many apps like this available now.

Collaboration is a great way to get your writing message out there. Working with bloggers, other authors, creatives, or with people who work within the theme of your book can be a positive experience. My novels are romances about businesswomen, so I could team up with a chocolatier, florist, holiday company offering romantic breaks, a business network, or hotel group, for example. Think outside the box and make connections. Keep in touch with your network regularly, even if it's just a quick note to say hello. This is where being part of a few groups helps, as you can engage with many people at once and save time for writing. Social networking does not have to take over your life. Pick what works for you and put the rest aside for later. If you try to do everything at once, you might exhaust yourself and have no space to stay creative. Believe you can achieve your dreams, and so will others. Don't undersell yourself. Work out what you need to charge for your time, not just to survive, but to prosper.

LET GO OF PROCRASTINATION. WRITE!

It can be difficult to keep yourself motivated and stop procrastinating when you are working alone, which is why networking can be so effective. Procrastination is a challenge we all face at one time or another and supporting each other can be crucial to our productivity. Some creatives prefer solitude, but for others it leaves us meandering along the street or gazing out of windows for hours without achieving anything. Perhaps this is because we are afraid of getting those words onto paper. If we do, the book or product becomes real, and we will end up having to show it to customers, if we want to sell any copies. This opens us up for criticism. What others think of our work can sometimes make or break our day! Creatives are also often their own worst critics.

Identify why you procrastinate. Social media can be very distracting. I bet if you timed how long you are on screen every day, it might surprise you. Use the productivity hacks mentioned in this book to keep yourself writing. Chatting to other writers can inspire us to get the words down, but it can also demoralise us if we begin comparing ourselves to others, so be careful to understand that we are all different and have various unique qualities to bring to our writing. Not everyone can write a bestseller – and not everyone wants to. Some writers long for a handful of readers, and that is their dream. Some authors have niche books that would always have a limited readership anyway. It doesn't have to deter them from finding their voice or their reading and writing community.

Procrastination is often a defence mechanism to avoid failure. There are ways to short cut it. Use a desk timer for writing sprints, or, as I have mentioned, find writing buddies at home or online to write alongside. Having a complete break and change of scenery from time to time can spark creativity. Writing a task list, that you can check off against, might also help. Have your writing goals, word counts and marketing performance aspirations written down. But remember to keep them realistic and achievable, or you could begin to de-motivate yourself again.

Research can also help with procrastination. If your research is done first, it can make work flow more easily, especially if your storyline is complicated and involves many characters. Some people are plotters, some pantsers (making up the story as they go along) and this might affect how prepared you are. I'm a definite pantser with my writing, but I still have detailed character sheets written out and brief chapter guidelines before I start, however vague they might be. This helps me know that the structure of the story will flow and that my characters won't jump from having blond hair to black, and green eyes to brown. It saves me time and energy, even though I often only have a rough idea of where my stories will take me until I'm writing them.

Write a first draft without editing. This can help your work to flow. No one manages a glitch-free story first time, so stop aiming for perfection and let your brain relax and enjoy the writing experience. It really is like nothing else, and it's something that fills my soul with joy and has become an absolute compulsion now. I can't wait to begin writing each day and carry notebooks practically everywhere, in case something inspires a new story.

You might also work faster when you are trying less hard, so let go of the idea of a perfect book for your first draft and get writing. Take out distractions or turn off social channels for a while. Writing time is different for everyone, and I know a lot of writers who can't just sit and write on demand. They need the freedom of having ideas sparked randomly, or need to write only when they feel like it. This can bring beautiful results too, so decide on your own preference. But take a minute to decide if you really should be doing whatever it is that is taking you away from your writing, or whether you are distracting yourself unnecessarily.

LOOK FOR MARKETING OPPORTUNITIES

I am always on the lookout for new ways to connect with people. I became a member of an amazing organisation for romance writers, called the *Romantic Novelist Association* or *RNA*. They run schemes to help new writers, but when I first published, I hadn't heard about them, unfortunately. There are groups like this for crime writers, such as the *Crime Writers' Association*, and for many other genres. You can find out about these groups via social media searches, or by word of mouth from other writers.

The *RNA* offers competitions for members to enter, it runs online book groups and it hosts gatherings and author talks, which are quite inspirational. They also plan conferences where you can spend a day, or even a few days, meeting other writers and adding to your network. These occasions are a fabulous way to build lasting friendships, discover people to work with, and connect with mentors who have lots of experience in the business of books and writing.

As I run my own popular book group on *Facebook*, I

offered my assistance with the new author and reader *Facebook* group that the *RNA* was trialling, which is now live. I'm currently an admin for that group too, which is a lot of fun. Please join if you love book groups. It's called The Romantic Fiction Book Club. I design their group graphics and get involved in running competitions. Through this group I've become friends with the other admins, who are such a brilliant and creative group of people, as well as being incredible writers. I've also met many new book lovers who have joined the group to share their latest reads. If you have the time, inspiration and energy, then offer to help people. You could be getting involved in something incredible.

The key with marketing opportunities is to be creative. There are lots of programmes and applications out there for you to try, many of which have free options.

Some of the sites I use:

- *Canva*. An easy way to make instant mock-ups for *Pinterest, Instagram, Facebook, Twitter* and others. It has set templates you can begin with and a free version to try.
- *Pixabay*. A free stock image site. Great for memes. If you use images in eBooks or print, please check permissions on each site.
- *Unsplash*. Free image site. Same rules apply for print. Check permissions.
- *Pexels*. Free image site. Same rules apply for print. Check permissions.
- *BookBrush*. An instant mock up and video site for quick book memes. Easy to create image ideas to make your book visible in a crowded market.

- *Tailwind.* A scheduling tool for *Pinterest.*
- *Hootsuite.* A great social media scheduling programme.
- *Buffer.* Another great social media scheduling service.
- *Kindlepreneur.* Fantastic book marketing applications and advice.

In today's digital age, it's very easy to use camera phones to snap either quick promotional photos of your book, or images to entertain your network. I often carry one or two of my books if I am travelling somewhere new, or even if I'm going somewhere locally, and then take some photos with my books there. I have managed to take some great images that are quite unusual! I couldn't believe my luck when I was visiting family at a Christmas market, and Batman and Darth Vader walked past. Never one to waste an opportunity, I asked them if I could take a picture of them holding my book. I absolutely love those photos and they didn't cost me anything to set up. One of my books is called *Ninja School Mum*, so it fitted the theme really well. Don't be afraid to ask politely for help. If it's not forthcoming, then say thanks anyway and move on to other ideas.

Both good reader photos and reviews are priceless. Encourage your readers to write reviews and use them in your marketing. Some reviewers might like to be asked for consent if you are actually adding their reviews to your books, but some adore being included. It's up to you to find out. You can use snippets from reviews in marketing, and it's a lot of fun to add them to book graphics and memes. This helps new readers see what others think about your work. Having photos featuring genuine readers is an added bonus. Add photos that readers have sent you to your social media.

This helps them feel involved in your writing career and creates content and interest for your timelines. It also shows that others have read and enjoyed your work.

I found a great way to encourage readers to send me photos of my books. I held an online book launch and ran a competition where participants were asked to send me a photo of their copies of my book to win a prize of another signed book and some book swag, which was a basket full of gifts. I asked for either a digital version, on their phones, iPads or Kindles, or a photo of the paperback, either with them or in a setting. It was a simple competition but it garnered so many great responses. This in turn gave me lots of lovely images of my book with readers – and put a huge smile on my face for days.

Book launches can be very simple or elaborate, and organising one can be quite a saga! Some authors only launch their books online, others enjoy a party with friends, family and readers. I have done both, and either way they are a good tool for network building. They take planning, but once you have developed a blueprint that works for you, you can use it time and time again. I held two of my book launches in big school libraries, as one of the books is set in a school playground, and the main character in the other is a teaching assistant who dreams of being a famous artist. This led to my books being stocked in school libraries, as well as a spot on the radio and local media interest. Look for venues appropriate to your books or genre when you plan your book launch. It's great to reach out to new audiences. Invite some of your network to attend your launches to create a buzz around your work.

Working together with other authors can help ease the pressures of constant marketing, and it can also be great fun. Here are some other ideas for collaborations that could help raise your book's profile:

- If you are working on joint promotions, share the workload: assign different jobs to each writer in a clear and concise manner, explaining in full how you will all benefit from each task.
- Combine talents: think about finding other authors who bring something different to the mix. One may have a great *Facebook* page, one a fantastic *Twitter* following, one may have contacts in the press and another might have a key relationship with wonderful book bloggers.
- Participation: don't just sit back and let others in the group do all the work. Contribute and network. Many bestselling authors run promotions together and they often work in the same market, not opposing ones. Although they are trying to attract similar readers, they are helping to broaden their market by having a greater reach.

A PROFESSIONAL APPROACH

The absolute key to finding readers is to write a good book. Everyone has a different view about what makes a good read – that's why there are so many popular genres. A fully edited, typeset, professional-looking book will be much more likely to catch a reader's eye than something with a poorly designed cover and lots of grammatical or formatting mistakes. Take your time to make your own book the absolute best it can be, especially if you are sending it out for submission to publishers or agents.

Make sure that your author branding is consistent, your posts are interesting and you are kind and courteous to your network. The connections you have made might be a handful of very enthusiastic friends and family who love your work, or a wider group of people, but whatever the size, there are always opportunities to broaden that network if you want to. Utilise the tips in this book to reach out to new contacts, connect with people who are like-minded and helpful, and can reciprocate by bringing skills or content that will benefit everyone.

My network has taken a long time to build. I've been

publishing books for eight years and many of my writing contacts have been made in the last two or three years. I'm still learning new skills, as we saw with *Pinterest* and the sudden jump and then decline in my unique views there, due to the time needed to create original and consistent pinning, and I will continue to experiment and schedule more time to enjoy the account. Small changes can have amazing results if you are willing to learn the skills to implement them.

I hope this book has been informative and that it gives you a real boost of enthusiasm to kick-start or continue your own writing career. Stay positive and focussed, and enjoy every minute of the writing journey that you are on. Keep writing!

If you have found this book beneficial, I would be really grateful if you could take a moment to leave a review or rating. Reviews help other readers to discover the book and you might be assisting a fellow writer on their journey to publication and beyond. Many thanks in advance! From Lizzie. Review link: viewbook.at/NetworkingForWriters

If you like interesting characters, laugh out loud storylines and sizzling locations, you'll love Lizzie Chantree's romance reads! Lizzie Chantree's book page.

CONNECT WITH LIZZIE ON SOCIAL MEDIA

lizziechantree.com

Twitter

Facebook

Lizzie's Book Group

Instagram

Pinterest

Goodreads

BookBub

LinkedIn

YouTube

Printed in Great Britain
by Amazon

48911122R00068